Copyright © 2021 Luna Peak Publishing
All rights reserved. No part of this publication may be reproduced, stored in any retrieval system or transmitted, in any form or by any means, electronic, mechanical, photocopying, recording or otherwise, without the prior permission of Luna Peak Publishing.

Luna Peak Publishing, Sierra Madre, California.
www.lunapeakpublishing.com

ISBN: 978-1-7355958-3-2
Printed and bound in the United States of America.
Cover art and design by Yolandi Oosthuizen.

KICKING CANCER

A MEMORY BOOK FOR KIDS

BY MELODY LOMBOY-LOWE

LUNA ▲▲ PEAK

Hey Little Fighter!

I have been where you are. It is a lot of hard work to be a cancer fighter. I was 6 years old when I was diagnosed with acute lymphoblastic leukemia. I had chemotherapy for 3 years and I was in the hospital too many times to count! Now I am all grown up, I have 3 kids of my own and I know how important it is to create and record memories.

I remember a lot from my time fighting cancer, but I wish I would have written my experiences in my own words and drawings. I created this book just for warriors like you! Please write down all of your feelings, your fears, your hopes and dreams. Have your friends sign this book and create a beautiful history book of this time. You are a cancer fighting machine- have fun filling out this workbook and stay strong!

Don't forget to celebrate life!

Love your fellow childhood cancer fighting friend,
Melody Lomboy-Lowe

This book belongs to:

_____

Nickname:

_____

Year:

_____

Diagnosis:

_____

Doctor's Name:

_____

Hospital:

_____

ABOUT THE AUTHOR

My name is _____

I am _____ years old.

I live in _____ CITY

I go to _____ SCHOOL

My siblings are

_____ NAMES

My parents are

_____ NAMES

MORE ABOUT ME!

COLOR ME

Favorite color _____

Favorite sport _____

Favorite friends

_____

Favorite foods

_____

Favorite TV shows

_____

TREATMENT PLAN!

What is your cancer called?

_____

What is your treatment?

_____

_____

How long will your treatment be?

_____

Make up a silly name for your cancer:

_____

CANCER  MONSTER

What do you think cancer would look like as a monster? Draw a cancer monster

YOU VS. CANCER

What do you think can defeat
the cancer monster? Draw yourself
defeating the cancer monster

What do you know about cancer?

FEELINGS WORD SEARCH

```
W S X Y Q Y Y D E F V O
W Q C Q J W E K C V W W
B M D A V I X M B Z O D
C E W E R B S K H T C L
E N P R S E H M E C J
X B O E D I D A W L J D
V W F L Q S R P W T C E
R E L A X E D P J Y T T
Q I G Z C D Q Y R E K I
J I T U I A L S N U I C
Y R G N A S K S Y T S X
J D U D Q F E G E J U E
```

Happy   Relaxed   Sad   Surprised   Angry
Excited Tense   Scared Worried   Love

How does chemotherapy make you feel?

_____
_____
_____
_____

Draw how you feel

Write a word for each letter of "cancer"

C _____

A _____

N _____

C _____

E _____

R _____

YOU ARE A STRONG CANCER FIGHTER!

Draw your strong body

During treatment you may need to stay inside at home a lot.
Draw your home

BORED AT HOME

Write about what you do when you are bored at home

_____
_____
_____
_____
_____
_____
_____
_____
_____

MY LIST OF HELPERS

Who is on your cancer support team?

- Doctor
- Nurses
- Family
- Friends

HOSPITAL WORD SEARCH

```
C Y F Z S G T I A E O M
K H D O C T O R B N A J
G J E D K V A L K I M A
S T D M Z O O M A C B W
N R N H O O K L P I U B
K U M E D T A I B D L C
K O R T M H P Z E A R
P K E S I T B E A M N S
Y S N P E S A O R D C H
T V S J A S G E S A E O
N O I T A I D A R K P T
H P U B U J Z B I T I Y
```

Nurse	Treatment	Chemotherapy	Medicine	Hospital
Doctor	Radiation	Ambulance	Blood Test	Shot

The hospital is where you receive treatment to heal your body.
Draw your hospital

WACKY HAIR DAY
Draw yourself with crazy hair

If you could have one visitor every day of the week, who would it be and why?

- Monday
- Tuesday
- Wednesday
- Thursday
- Friday
- Saturday
- Sunday

BORED AT THE HOSPITAL

Write about what you do when you are bored at the hospital

_____
_____
_____
_____
_____
_____
_____
_____

HOSPITAL MEMORIES

Write about a fun time
in the hospital

_____
_____
_____
_____
_____
_____
_____
_____

How did you feel when you first heard that you had cancer?

_____

_____

_____

_____

Draw how you feel

Have you learned any new skills since you were diagnosed? Draw them!

LET'S EAT!

What are your favorite foods to eat?
What are your least favorite foods?
Draw or write about them!

DESIGN A MASK!

Do you wear a mask to stay healthy after treatment? Design your own mask!

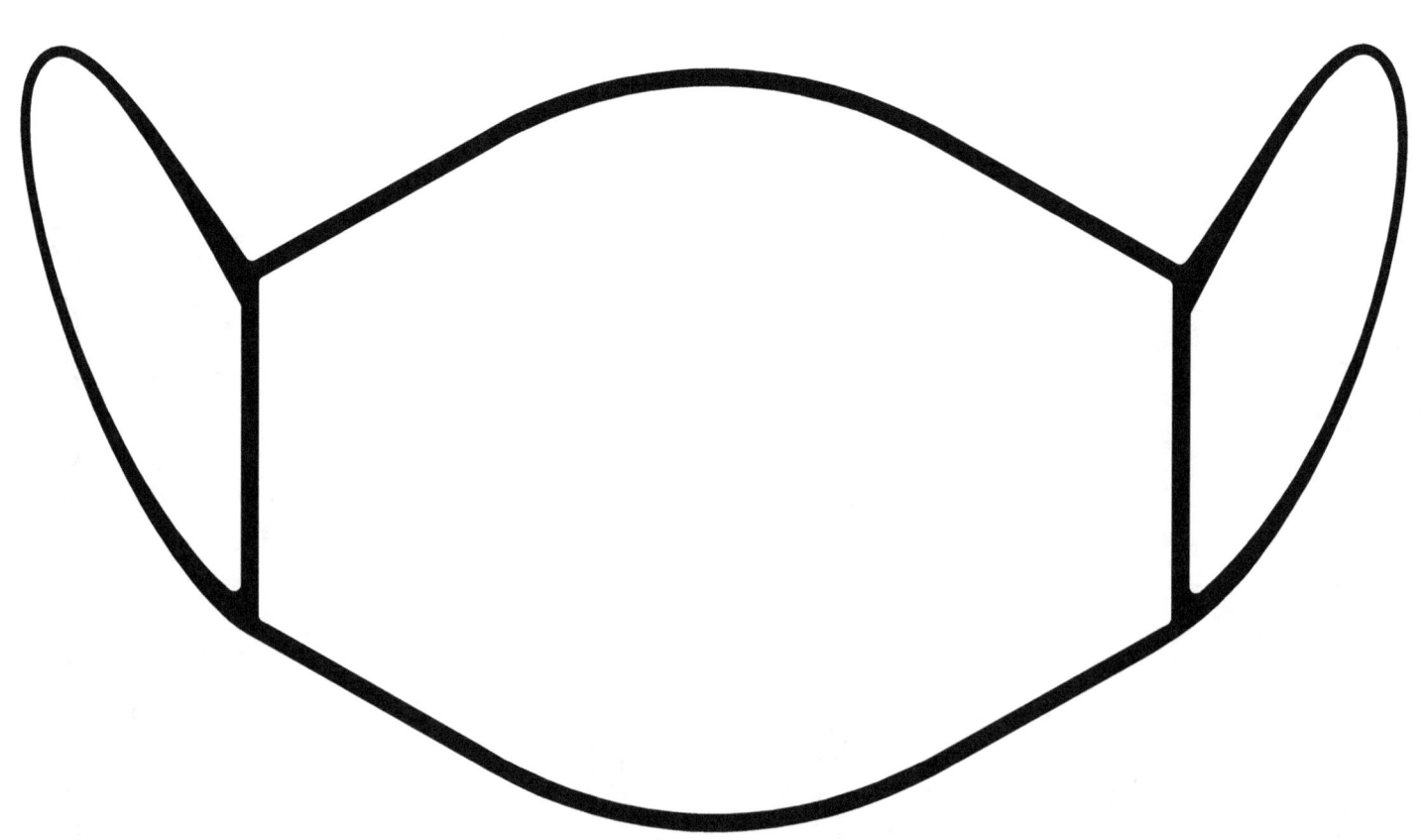

Are you still going to school? What do you miss the most about school?

Draw your school

THE NEW YOU!

What is different now after having cancer? Write what you have learned

_____

_____

_____

_____

_____

_____

_____

_____

_____

MY FAMILY!

What has your family been doing differently since cancer?

_____
_____
_____
_____
_____
_____
_____
_____
_____
_____

HOPE WORD SEARCH

```
R Z X B P A S C X K E J
C U J E H A O J H T T Z
P A G H W A S B O N F S
E O Y T O D P F P P W E
M T V A N D J P E Z G H
C C A E L D Z E Y I Z J
C Y I R H S I W F V P G
N R A B B I W T J T E X
F Q B L H E P R M L B R
T G F Z P T L W X N L Y
F A M I L Y O E A U T L
C X C U J E X N C F T Q
```

....

Breathe	Happy	Fun	Celebrate	Gift
Friends	Wish	Hope	Family	Play

Who makes you feel better when you feel sad, and why?

Their name: _____

THINGS I CAN
DO TO FEEL HAPPY

1. _____

2. _____

3. _____

4. _____

5. _____

PERFECT DAY IN!

Write about your perfect day inside your house

Don't touch your eyes, nose or mouth.
WHY?

_____

HAND WASHING

Why is it important to wash your hands often?

_____

Draw germs on the hands

What **SCARY** things have happened to you?

_____

_____

_____

_____

Draw how you feel

What **EXCITING** things have happened to you?

_____

_____

_____

_____

Draw how you feel

SUPER ME

Write about if you were a super hero fighting cancer

What is your superhero name?
_____

What is your super power?
_____

How do you fight cancer?
_____

AFTER TREATMENT WORD SEARCH

```
P F P R P P F T V M Y T
R J V L O E R U C J H L
I I Z W I I A A Y H T S
D C E L C Y R C P B L L
E R E M O O D R E F A K
M R S T R O N G A P E Q
D E H S I N I F Y W H A
H I C Y W Y N X D O O M
Z M H I N W E U Y Q J F
T B L Q H I G O V Z U V
T J F Y F T A Q Z I D F
V F G N B E Q A F C U Z
```

Pride   Healthy   Strong   Cure   Peace
Warrior   Power   Joy   Finished   Relief

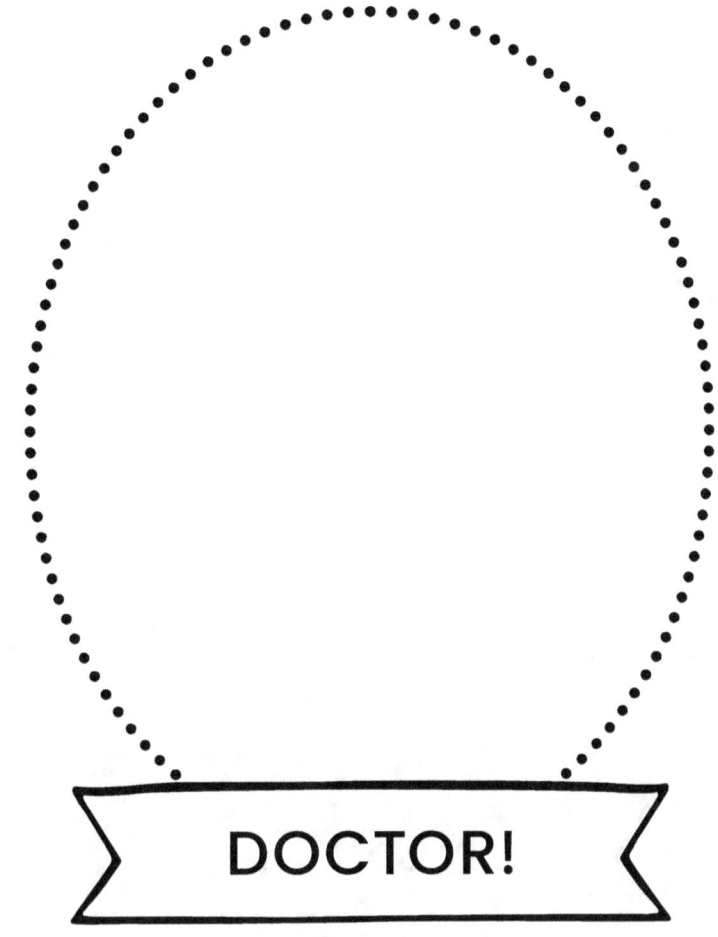

DOCTOR!

Who is your favorite doctor?
Draw or write about them!

_____
_____
_____
_____

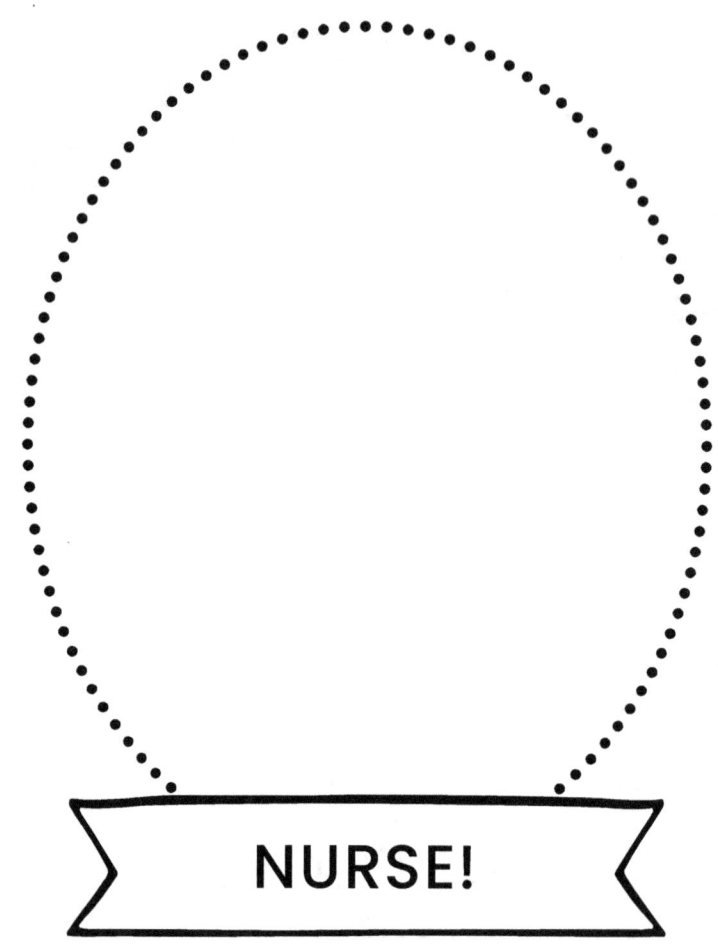

NURSE!

Who is your favorite nurse?
Draw or write about them!

_____

_____

_____

_____

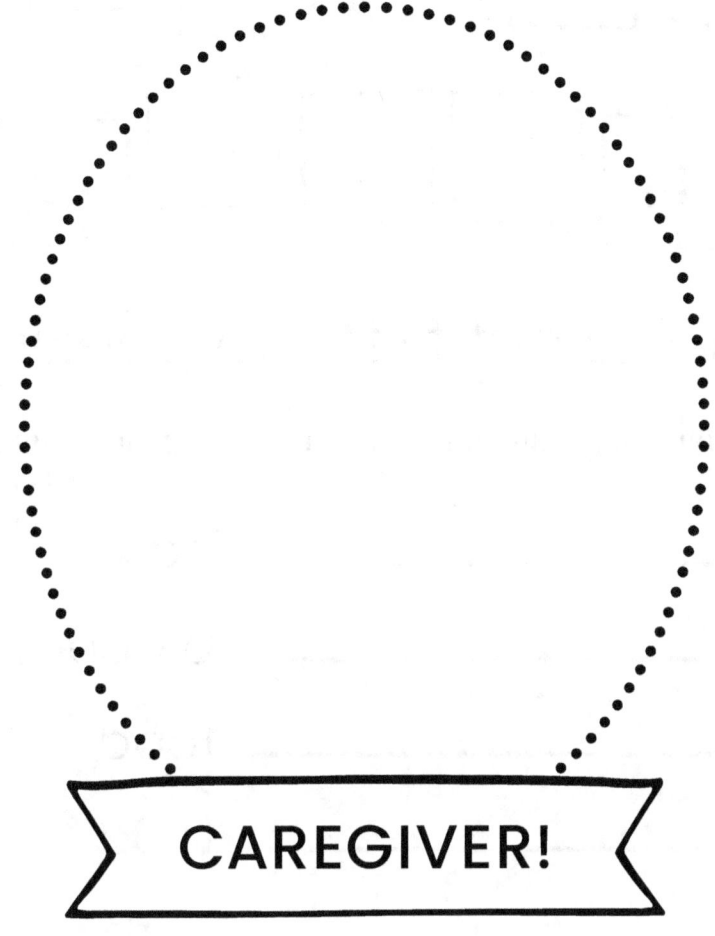

CAREGIVER!

Who is your favorite caregiver?
Draw or write about them!

_____
_____
_____
_____

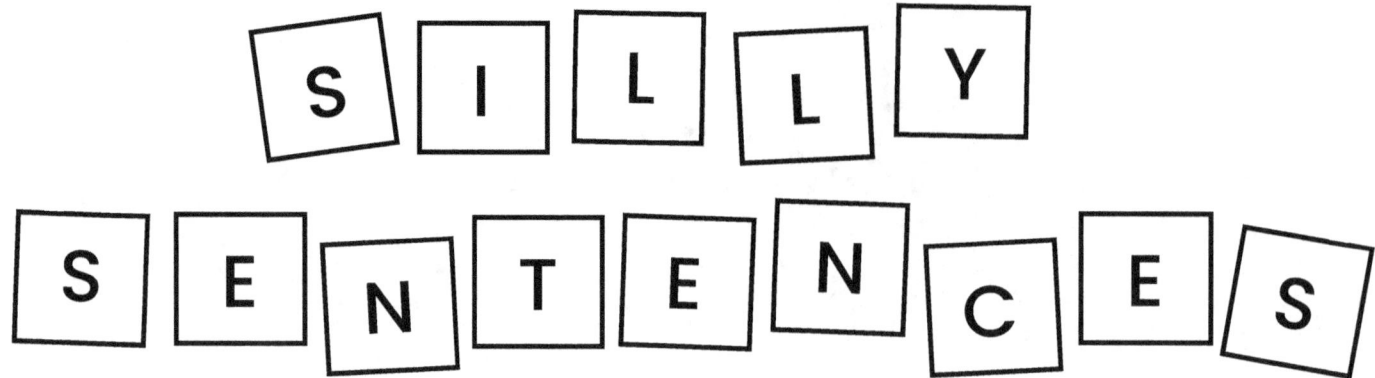

Fill this out first! No peeking.

1. _____ name
2. _____ place
3. _____ food
4. _____ food
5. _____ verb
6. _____ number
7. _____ body part
8. _____ noun
9. _____ vehicle
10. _____ friend
11. _____ friend
12. _____ verb (past tense)

SILLY SENTENCES

13. _____ social media app

14. _____ number

15. _____ number

16. _____ sport

17. _____ noun

18. _____ costume

19. _____ clothing

20. _____ family member

21. _____ food

22. _____ family member

23. _____ song

24. _____ family member

25. _____ animal

26. _____ feeling

27. _____ feeling

28. _____ feeling

SILLY SENTENCES

Fill out your answers from the previous page!

THE BEST DAY EVER

One day my best friend, 1_____
                          NAME

and I went to 2_____. We needed
                 PLACE

a fun day together. For breakfast I ate

3_____ topped with 4_____.
    FOOD   FOOD

It was so delicious that I started to

5_____ up and down in my chair.
    VERB

My best friend thought it was funny so I did

SILLY SENTENCES

it 6 _____ more times. But it made
      NUMBER

my 7 _____ hurt and I almost threw
      BODY PART

up in the 8 _____. It was crazy!
            NOUN

After breakfast we took the 9 _____
                              VEHICLE

for a ride around the neighborhood. We

saw 10 _____ and 11 _____
       FRIEND   FRIEND

and they 12 _____ for us and we
            VERB (PAST TENSE)

recorded it for 13 _____. It got
                   SOCIAL MEDIA APP

14 _____ likes in 15 _____
   NUMBER   NUMBER

minutes! After that we decided to go to

the beach and play 16 _____ in
                      SPORT

the ocean! The lifeguards thought it was

SILLY SENTENCES

funny when we made a 17 _____
                         NOUN

in the sand and dressed it in a

18 _____. I decided to jump into
   COSTUME

the ocean but my 19 _____ got
                    CLOTHING

wet! So we ran home to get changed

and then my 20 _____ served us
               FAMILY MEMBER

21 _____ for lunch.
   FOOD

SILLY SENTENCES

Finally we decided to finish the day off by inviting all of our friends and family over for a Celebration of Life party. My 22 _____ (FAMILY MEMBER) sang their favorite song 23 _____ (SONG) and my 24 _____ (FAMILY MEMBER) danced like a 25 _____ (ANIMAL). We loved all being together and decided to do this every year to celebrate. I felt 26 _____ (FEELING) and 27 _____ (FEELING) and 28 _____ (FEELING) and I want to feel that way for many years. I cannot wait for the next Celebration of Life party!

SILLY SENTENCES

Fill this out first! No peeking.

1. _____ adjective
2. _____ noun
3. _____ adjective
4. _____ verb ending in -ing
5. _____ noun (plural)
6. _____ adjective
7. _____ family member
8. _____ adjective
9. _____ noun (plural)
10. _____ adjective
11. _____ noun
12. _____ noun

13. _____ noun
14. _____ vehicle
15. _____ verb
16. _____ noun
17. _____ noun
18. _____ noun (plural)
19. _____ city
20. _____ celebrity
21. _____ celebrity
22. _____ adjective
23. _____ adjective
24. _____ noun
25. _____ noun
26. _____ noun
27. _____ color
28. _____ body part
29. _____ number
30. _____ noun
31. _____ name
32. _____ noun

SILLY SENTENCES

Fill out your answers from the previous page!

SUPER HERO

Today was the 1 _____ day of my
                    ADJECTIVE

entire life! When I woke up in the morning,

I was just a 2 _____ like everyone
                 NOUN

else. Then I found out a 3 _____
                              ADJECTIVE

secret. I was 4 _____ through a
                  VERB ENDING IN -ING

secret chest where my family keeps all of

our 5 _____ and I found a picture
       NOUN (PLURAL)

SILLY SENTENCES

of my family wearing 6_____
                        ADJECTIVE

capes. I asked 7_____ why they
                  FAMILY MEMBER

had dressed like that and they told me

the 8_____ truth. We are a family
       ADJECTIVE

of 9_____! My family wanted
     NOUN (PLURAL)

to get away from the 10_____
                          ADJECTIVE

life, but they said I can live my life like a

11_____ if I want to. I yelled, "Yes!"
   NOUN

Now that I'm a super 12_____, I
                          NOUN

need a 13_____. I'm not going
          NOUN

to drive a 14_____ anymore.
              VEHICLE

We all have to fly, leap, teleport, or

SILLY SENTENCES

15 _____ instead. I'll never have
   VERB

to take out the 16 _____ or
                    NOUN

wash the 17 _____ ever again.
            NOUN

Maybe the president will ask me to save

18 _____ in 19 _____. And
   NOUN (PLURAL)   CITY

since 20 _____ and 21 _____
         CELEBRITY   CELEBRITY

are both evil, I'll invite them to my

22 _____ lair for a 23 _____
   ADJECTIVE   ADJECTIVE

dinner, defeat them, and save the world.

The world will declare

SILLY SENTENCES

me the 24 _____ superhero of
          NOUN

the universe. They will make a statue of

me holding a 25 _____ in the air.
                NOUN

I'll have my own television show called

the biggest 26 _____. Everywhere
               NOUN

I go, I'll walk the 27 _____ carpet
                      COLOR

and wave my 28 _____ at my fans.
                BODY PART

I'll have 29 _____ followers on my
             NUMBER

social 30 _____ page. I love being
          NOUN

a superhero! My name, 31 _____
                          NAME

the super-32 _____ will go
              NOUN

down in history.

CELEBRATE LIFE!

Draw a picture of yourself, healthy and happy

Notes from my doctors

Notes from my nurses

Notes from my caregivers

Notes from my family

Notes from my friends

YOUR JOURNAL

Diagnosis Date

_____ , _____ , _____
MONTH   DAY   YEAR

Treatment Started

_____ , _____ , _____
MONTH   DAY   YEAR

Treatment Ended

_____ , _____ , _____
MONTH   DAY   YEAR

Make sure to always date your journal entries. This is your memory book of this historical time.

DATE _____

DATE _____

DATE _____

_____
_____
_____
_____
_____
_____

DATE _____

_____
_____
_____
_____
_____
_____

DATE _____

_____

_____

_____

_____

_____

_____

DATE _____

_____

_____

_____

_____

_____

_____

DATE _____

_____
_____
_____
_____
_____
_____

DATE _____

_____
_____
_____
_____
_____
_____

DATE _____

DATE _____

DATE _____

DATE _____

DATE _____

_____
_____
_____
_____
_____
_____

DATE _____

_____
_____
_____
_____
_____
_____

DATE _____

_____
_____
_____
_____
_____
_____

DATE _____

_____
_____
_____
_____
_____
_____

DATE _____

_____
_____
_____
_____
_____
_____

DATE _____

_____
_____
_____
_____
_____
_____

DATE _____

DATE _____

www.ingramcontent.com/pod-product-compliance
Lightning Source LLC
Chambersburg PA
CBHW081406070526
44583CB00020B/2697